Everyone is a leader to someone.
Whether that someone be an employee
(or thousands of employees),
your spouse, a child, or
at the simplest level, oneself;
you are a leader.

~ TRACY BRINKMANN

LEADERSHIP
LESSONS

Powerful Quotes & Inspiring Messages…

for everyone

Compiled and Written

by

ERIC HARVEY & STEVE VENTURA

To order additional copies of this book, or for information
on other WALK THE TALK® products and services,
contact us at **1.888.822.9255**
or visit **www.walkthetalk.com**

LEADERSHIP LESSONS

Printed in the United States of America
10 9 8 7 6 5 4 3 2 1

Edited by Tonda Agold
Designed and Printed by Branch Smith

ISBN-13: 978-1-885228-89-5
ISBN-10: 1-885228-89-9

$12.95

90000

9 781885 228895

INTRODUCTION

If you think "leadership" is a concept
that only applies to certain
people in business, governmental,
and civic organizations, think again!
Fact is – no matter our age, gender,
occupation, education level, or station
in life – each of us touches
and influences other lives …
each of us is a leader to
someone.

Certainly, that "someone" can be an employee (or a group of employees) we might supervise at work. But it can also be a coworker we interact with or a customer we serve … a spouse we honor or a child we nurture … a relative we care for or a friend we care about … a student we teach or a player we coach … a fellow member of our church, club, league, or association … or anyone for whom we have made a positive difference through our actions and example.

That's why LEADERSHIP is something we all must be concerned with. That's why the lessons presented in this book apply to each of us … that's why they apply to YOU.

Throughout the pages that follow, you'll find a collection of inspirational quotations from statesmen, military figures, business executives, writers, poets, athletes, and well-known celebrities – along with thought-provoking ideas and strategies that we've garnered over the years – all intended to enhance your understanding of the *essence* of leadership.

Pay attention to what you're about to read. Think about the words you see and the messages they convey. More importantly, focus on how you can *apply* those messages in order to improve your life and the lives of others.

Your "someone" is counting on you for leadership. Don't let him, her, or them down.

TABLE OF CONTENTS

Leadership is ...

Leadership is …

LISTENING

*The roots of effective leadership lie
in simple things, one of which is listening.
Listening to someone demonstrates respect;
it shows that you value their ideas and are
willing to hear them.*

~ JOHN BALDONI

One of the best ways to persuade others is with your ears.

~ Dean Rusk

Listening, not imitation, may be the sincerest form of flattery.

~ Dr. Joyce Brothers

One often hears the remark, "He talks too much," but when did anyone last hear the criticism, "He listens too much"?

~ Norman Augustine

One who cares is one who listens.

~ Richard Clarke

Every person I work with knows something better than me.
My job is to listen long enough to find it and use it.

~ Jack Nichols

Nature has given us two ears, two eyes,
and but one tongue – to the end that we should hear
and see more than we speak.

~ Socrates

I remind myself every morning: Nothing I say this day
will teach me anything. So if I'm going to learn,
I must do it by listening.

~ Larry King

The greatest compliment
that was ever paid me
was when one asked me
what I thought,
and attended to my answer.

~ Henry David Thoreau

Leadership is …

LOYALTY

The best things in life are never rationed.

Friendship, loyalty, love do not

require coupons.

~ GEORGE T. HEWITT

Leadership is a two-way street, loyalty up and loyalty down.
Respect for one's superiors; care for one's crew.

~ Adm. Grace Murray Hopper

An ounce of loyalty is worth a pound of cleverness.

~ Elbert Hubbard

Loyalty is something you give regardless
of what you get back, and in giving loyalty,
you're getting more loyalty; and out of loyalty
flow other great qualities.

~ Charles "Tremendous" Jones

You've got to give loyalty down, if you want loyalty up.

~ Donald T. Regan

There are no secrets to success.
Don't waste your time looking for them.
Success is the result of perfection,
hard work, learning from failure, loyalty
to those for whom you work,
and persistence.

~ Gen. Colin Powell

Unless you can find some sort of loyalty, you cannot
find unity and peace in your active living.

~ Josiah Royce

The "3 P's" of Leadership LOYALTY

Leaders are loyal to …

The **PEOPLE** they work with and for,
The **PURPOSE** they serve,
The **PRINCIPLES** they hold dear.

ARE YOU THE ANSWER?

If others were to ask "What ever happened to loyalty?"

would they be able to point at you and say:

"It's alive and well … right there!"?

Leadership is …

LOOKING OUT
FOR OTHERS

A good leader is a caring leader –
he not only cares about his people, he actively
takes care of them.

~ HARALD ANDERSON

We're here for a reason. I believe a bit of
the reason is to throw little torches out to lead
people through the dark.

~ Whoopi Goldberg

A leader is someone who helps improve
the lives of other people or improve
the system they live under.

~ Sam Ervin, Jr.

These three rules are all you need, whether you are a coach,
a player, a parent, a child, an employer, or an employee.
Everyone you meet asks three questions mentally:

1. Can I trust you?
2. Are you committed to excellence?
3. Do you care about me?

~ Lou Holtz

No man can persuade people to do what he wants
them to do unless he genuinely likes people and
believes that what he wants them to do is to their
own advantage.

~ Bruce Barton

It doesn't matter who or where you are, or how
successful you become in a worldly way ... in a
corporate board room, in a hospital operating theater,
setting public policy, or managing your private life ...
you must care for other people.

~ Barbara Bush

Too often we underestimate the power
of a touch, a smile, a kind word, a listening ear, an
honest compliment, or the smallest act
of caring, all of which have the potential to turn
a life around.

~ Leo Buscaglia

No one cares how much you know

until they know how much you care!

Leadership is ...

ENDURANCE

Leaders must be self-reliant individuals

with great tenacity and stamina.

~ THOMAS E. CRONIN

Pain is temporary. Quitting lasts forever.

~ Lance Armstrong

Press on. Nothing in the world can take
the place of persistence. Talent will not;
nothing is more common than unsuccessful men
with talent. Genius will not; unrewarded genius
is almost a proverb. Education will not; the world
is full of educated derelicts. Persistence and
determination alone are omnipotent.

~ Calvin Coolidge

It's not whether you get knocked down,
it's whether you get up.

~ Vince Lombardi

We can do anything we want to if we
stick to it long enough.

~ Helen Keller

If Columbus had turned back, no one would
have blamed him. Of course, no one would
have remembered him either.

~ Unknown

It takes twenty years to become an overnight success.

~ Eddie Cantor

Exceptional Endurance

At age 22 – He failed in business

At age 23 – He ran for the Legislature and was defeated

At age 24 – He failed in business, once again

At age 25 – He finally was elected to the Legislature

but then ...

At age 29 – He was defeated for Speaker of the House

At age 34 – He was defeated for Congress

At age 39 – He lost another bid for Congress

At age 46 – He was defeated for the Senate

At age 47 – He was defeated for Vice President

At age 49 – He was again defeated for the Senate

however ...

At age 51 – He was elected President of the United States

He was ...
Abraham Lincoln

Leadership is …

EMPOWERMENT

*The task of leadership is not to put
greatness into people, but to elicit it, for the
greatness is there already.*

~ JOHN BUCHAN

A good leader inspires others with confidence in him;
a great leader inspires them with confidence in themselves.

~ Unknown

As a leader … your principal job is to create an operating
environment where others can do great things.

~ Richard Teerlink

Don't tell people how to do things, tell them what to do
and let them surprise you with their results.

~ Gen. George S. Patton

Outstanding leaders go out of their way to boost
the self-esteem of their personnel. If people believe
in themselves, it's amazing what they can accomplish.

~ Sam Walton

You have to enable and empower people to make
decisions independent of you. As I've learned, each
person on a team is an extension of your leadership;
if they feel empowered by you they will magnify
your power to lead.

~ Tom Ridge

No [person] will make a great leader who wants to do
it all himself, or to get all the credit for doing it.

~ Andrew Carnegie

When the best leader's
work is done,
the people say
"We did it ourselves!"

~ Lao Tzu

BE A LEADER ...

A boss creates fear,

a **leader** confidence.

A boss fixes blame,

a **leader** corrects mistakes.

A boss knows all,

a **leader** asks questions.

A boss makes work drudgery,

a **leader** makes it interesting.

A boss is interested in himself or herself,

a **leader** is interested in the group.

~ RUSSELL H. EWING

... NOT A "BOSS"

The **boss** drives people;

the leader coaches them.

The **boss** depends on authority;

the leader on good will.

The **boss** inspires fear;

the leader inspires enthusiasm.

The **boss** says "I"; the leader says "WE".

The **boss** fixes blame for the breakdown;

the leader fixes the breakdown.

The **boss** says, "GO";

the leader says "LET'S GO!"

~ GORDON SELFRIDGE

Leadership is ...

EXAMPLE

If your actions inspire others to dream more,

learn more, do more and become more,

you are a leader.

~ JOHN QUINCY ADAMS

As I grow older, I pay less attention to what men say.
I just watch what they do.

~ Andrew Carnegie

If you are given a chance to be a role model, I think
you should always take it because you can influence
a person's life in a positive light, and that's what I
want to do. That's what it's all about.

~ Tiger Woods

Leadership is a matter of having people look at you
and gain confidence, seeing how you react. If you're
in control, they're in control.

~ Tom Landry

A leader is one who knows the way, goes
the way and shows the way.

~ John C. Maxwell

Example is not the main thing in influencing others,
it is the only thing.

~ Albert Schweitzer

What you are will show in what you do.

~ Thomas A. Edison

Leadership by example is the only kind of real leadership.
Everything else is dictatorship.

~ Albert Emerson Unaterra

The first great gift we can bestow on
others is a good example.

~ Thomas Morell

Be the change you want to see in the world.

~ Mahatma Gandhi

This, then, is the test we must set for ourselves;
not to march alone but to march in such a way
that others will wish to join us.

~ Hubert H. Humphrey

Leadership is …

ATTITUDE

*There is little difference in people,
but that little difference makes a big difference.
That little difference is attitude. The big difference is
whether it is positive or negative.*

~ W. CLEMENT STONE

Leadership is practiced not so much in
words as in attitude and in actions.

~ Harold Geneen

Ability is what you're capable of doing.
Motivation determines what you do.
Attitude determines how well you do it.

~ Lou Holtz

It is your attitude, not your aptitude, that
determines your altitude.

~ Zig Ziglar

HOW YOU CHOOSE TO SEE THINGS ...

Three men were laboring in a field of boulders and large stones. Sweat ran from their foreheads as they swung their heavy picks again and again.

A curious passer-by approached the men and asked each what he was doing.

The first man answered in a stern and abrupt voice:

Can't you see, I'm breaking rocks!

The second man replied in a matter-of-fact way:

Can't you see, I'm earning my salary!

The third man smiled – his eyes gleaming with enthusiasm – and proclaimed:

Can't you see, I'm helping to build a cathedral!

The longer I live, the more I realize the impact of attitude
on life. Attitude, to me, is more important than facts.
It is more important than the past, than education, than
money, than circumstances, than failure, than successes,
than what other people think or say or do. It is more important than
appearance, giftedness or skill. It will make or break
a company, a church, a home.

The remarkable thing is we have a choice every day
regarding the attitude we will embrace for that day.
We cannot change our past ... we cannot change the fact
that people will act in a certain way. We cannot change the
inevitable. The only thing we can do is play on the one string
we have, and that is our attitude. I am convinced that life is
10% what happens to me and 90% how I react to it.

~ Charles Swindoll

Leadership is …

ACTION

*Don't lose sight of the most important factors
that lead to successful leadership: commitment,
a passion to make a difference, a vision for achieving
positive change, and the courage to take action.*

~ LARRAINE MATUSAK

Do something. If it works, do more of it.
If it doesn't, do something else.

~ Franklin D. Roosevelt

Someone's sitting in the shade today because
someone planted a tree a long time ago.

~ Warren Buffett

You don't lead by pointing and telling people some
place to go. You lead by going to that place
and making a case.

~ Ken Kesey

Leadership is action, not position.

~ Donald H. McGannon

Even if you are on the right track,
you will get run over if you just sit there.

~ Will Rogers

Apply yourself. Get all the education you can,
but then, by God, do something. Don't just stand there,
make it happen.

~ Lee Iacocca

I think I'll never run out of things to accomplish,
as long as I'm alive, because there's so much to learn,
and so much to do. I always feel like I have so much further
to go, personally, spiritually, emotionally, mentally,
and physically.

~ Queen Latifah

Not all actions are right and appropriate. Here are some

ACTIONS THAT EFFECTIVE LEADERS AVOID

Jumping to conclusions

Passing the buck

Grabbing the credit

Throwing your weight around

Stretching the truth

Breaking your promises

Playing favorites

Stepping on others

Plugging your ears

Side-stepping problems

Spreading rumors and discontent

Holding others back

Pressing "my way or the highway"

Just *skating* by

Looking out only for "number one"

Leadership is …

AUTHORITY

Nearly all men can stand adversity, but if you want to test a man's character, give him power.

~ ABRAHAM LINCOLN

You do not lead by hitting people over the head –
that's assault, not leadership.

~ Dwight D. Eisenhower

A good leader takes a little more than his share of the
blame, a little less than his share of the credit.

~ Arnold H. Glasgow

Being powerful is like being a lady. If you have to
tell people you are, you aren't.

~ Margaret Thatcher

Leadership is not about being important,
it's about serving something important.

~ Vanna Bonta

Leadership is …

DEPENDABILITY

*If you really want people to respond
to your leadership, you have to have a
personal relationship with them. They need
to know you're dependable and that you'll
be there if they have a problem.*

~ NOREEN HAFFNER

The greatest ability is dependability.

~ Bob Jones

All successful leaders place a premium on
keeping their promises and commitments.
If they say they'll do something –
whether important or seemingly insignificant –
they remember it … and they DO it.
They count on the fact that people
can count on them.

~ *LEAD RIGHT*

Leaders must be dependable people –
ALL THE TIME!

~ Charles C. Krulak

Leadership is …

DETERMINATION

*You've got to get up every morning
with determination if you're going to
go to bed with satisfaction.*

~ GEORGE LORIMER

Nothing of worth or weight can be achieved
with half a mind, with a faint heart,
and with a lame endeavor.

~ Isaac Barrow

A leader has the vision and conviction that a
dream can be achieved. He inspires the power
and energy to get it done.

~ Ralph Lauren

To be a leader, you must stand for something,
or you will fall for anything.

~ Anthony Pagano

There are no office hours for leaders.

~ Cardinal J. Gibbons

If you want to be comfortable, take an easy job.
If you aspire to leadership, take off your coat.

~ Unknown

Whenever anything is being accomplished,
it is being done, I have learned, by a
monomaniac with a mission.

~ Peter Drucker

Of all the things a leader should fear,
complacency heads the list.

~ John C. Maxwell

Good enough never is.

~ Debbi Fields

ARE YOU THE ANSWER?

If others were to ask
"Do determination and commitment still exist?"
would they be able to point at you and say:
"YES … they surely do!"?

Leadership is …

DEVELOPING
OTHERS

*The growth and development of people
is the highest calling of leadership.*

~ HARVEY S. FIRESTONE

Before you are a leader, success is all
about growing yourself. When you become a
leader, success is all about growing others.

~ Jack Welch

A leader's skill is best rated not by how
smoothly things run while you're there, but
by how well they go after you have left.

~ Sally Helgesen

What really matters is not just our own winning
but helping other people to win, too.

~ Fred Rogers

Give a man a fish, and you feed him for a day.
Teach a man to fish, and you feed him for a lifetime.

~ Chinese Proverb

Probably my best quality as a coach is that I ask
a lot of challenging questions and let the
person come up with the answer.

~ Phil Dixon

The ultimate leader is one who is willing to
develop people to the point that they surpass
him or her in knowledge and ability.

~ Fred A. Manske, Jr.

If there is anything I would like to
be remembered for it is that I helped
people understand that leadership is helping
other people grow and succeed.
To repeat myself, leadership is not just
about you. It's about them.

~ Jack Welch

LEADERSHIP IN ACTION

Kayla Brown was barely out of college, in her first teaching job, when she made a discovery that would change her life … and the lives of many others.

One delightful and bright kindergarten student – whose usual happy demeanor and eagerness to learn were a joy to Brown – suddenly changed. Despite her best efforts, no amount of coaxing or correcting could shake the boy from this change in personality. Then one day, when Brown was on cafeteria duty, she heard a group of children laughing.

They were laughing at the little boy.

"I walked over closer to the table, and he was licking his plate," Brown said. The child was holding the plate in front of him and licking it – paying little attention to the laughter around him. She thought he was being silly or playing for attention until she moved closer and looked into the eyes of an intensely sad child. When questioned about the behavior, the boy merely said, "I'm hungry."

Brown learned that the boy's father had abandoned the family —
leaving them with no money and no food in the house. She went
to her church and was able to arrange help for the mother and
her children.

That seemed like enough of a fix until she moved to a new school
in Bowie, Texas, where there was a higher proportion of children
living in poverty. There, she discovered the same problem: irritable
and poor-performing students who were just hungry.

She went to her pastor and got her new church involved in supple-
menting the children's meals. Brown, along with a group of church
and school volunteers, started packaging food for approximately
170 children … every weekend.

The project became known as Backpack Buddies because teachers
quietly slipped the food into children's backpacks while they were
at recess.

Source: ABC News

Leadership is …

EMPATHY

*Successful leaders lead with the heart,
not just the head. They possess qualities
like empathy, compassion and courage.*

~ BILL GEORGE

There are a lot of brilliant people in this world who are,
and will remain, ineffective leaders … they are so
interested in themselves and their own accomplishments
that they never get around to appreciating and
understanding the feelings of the other people.

Sometimes, usually later in life, these talented, egocentric
individuals suffer painful hardships. They understand,
often for the first time, the kind of problems less talented
or less fortunate people have suffered all their lives. They
suddenly discover a new and important dimension: sensitivity
to the feelings, emotions, and experiences of other people.

Effective leaders don't wait for life to bring them to
their knees before they appreciate the kind of problems
others are facing. Instead they constantly try to put
themselves in others' shoes – try to imagine how
they would feel in the same circumstances.

~ John Luther
(abridged)

The great gift of human beings is that we have
the power of empathy.

~ Meryl Streep

You never really understand a person until you
consider things from his point of view – until you
climb inside of his skin and walk around in it.

~ Atticus Finch, *To Kill a Mockingbird*

I believe that we all do the best we can in every
situation. Understanding this, it helps me look
with compassion on others, especially when
I think they're screwing up.

~ John Woods

QUESTIONS THAT
EMPATHETIC LEADERS ASK

How are my actions affecting others?

What issues / problems is he or she dealing with?

How would I feel / react if this were happening to me?

Have I done my best to create a "win-win" outcome?

What will it take for others to support my ideas and plans?

*What can I do to help others deal with any
challenges they may be facing?*

What can I do to show others that I care about them?

Leadership is ...

EXPECTATIONS

*It is the nature of man
to rise to greatness if
greatness is expected of him.*

~ JOHN STEINBECK

Children are likely to live up to
what you believe of them.

~ Lady Bird Johnson

Let us be about setting high standards for life, love,
creativity, and wisdom. If our expectations in these
areas are low, we are not likely to experience
wellness. Setting high standards makes every day and
every decade worth looking forward to.

~ Greg Anderson

Whether you think that you can or that
you can't, you are usually right.

~ Henry Ford

I don't think anything is unrealistic if you
believe you can do it.

~ Mike Ditka

To whom much is given, much is expected.

~ multiple sources

THE SELF-FULFILLING PROPHECY

When you expect things to happen –

whether good or bad – you tend to act in ways

that make them more likely to actually occur.

Expect the best from yourself and others and

you increase the odds that you'll get it.

LEADERSHIP IN ACTION

After entering the hospital and taking the elevator to the proper floor, NFL coach Don Shula walked down the hallway and entered a numbered room. He moved toward the bandaged figure on the bed.

The patient recognized him, smiled as best he could, and raised an arm from which several tubes dangled.

Thanks for coming, coach.

How you doing? inquired Shula.

Oh, okay replied the bed-ridden man whose mournful look told a much different story.

There was a long pause as the two men looked at each other. Finally, Shula leaned in – his prominent jaw jutting close to the patient's face.

Listen, Mike, I need you in training camp in July – on the field, ready to go. We're going all the way this year.

After recovering from bone cancer, Mike Westhoff, still the special-teams coach for the Miami Dolphins, said of Shula:

I thought he would tuck me in, but he didn't. He treated me the way I could be, not the way I was.

~ Adapted from an article in *Success* magazine

Leadership is …

EVERYONE'S JOB

*Whether we are called upon to be involved in
leading government or business, guiding young
minds, leading a family, standing for what is right,
or organizing a dinner, a carpool, or a household,
everyone has a leadership role to play.*

~ MICHAEL MCKINNEY

Leaders … we tend to think of them as business owners, CEO's, and managers at all levels. Traditionally, leadership also extends into politics and other global affairs. However, parents, therapists and health care providers … sports coaches, consultants, mentors, partners in relationship, teachers, authors, and others who interact with people on a regular basis are all leaders. Everyone is a leader either by choice or default.

~ Bruce D. Schneider

Everyone is a leader in his or her organization. Even if you don't hold a titled leadership position, such as supervisor, manager, human resource director, or CEO, you still have many opportunities every day through your actions and behavior to model leadership qualities.

~ Connie Podesta

LEADERS ARE KNOWN BY MANY LABELS ...

"Manager"	"Parent"	"Teacher"
"Student"	"Coach"	"Scout"
"Captain"	"Involved Citizen"	"Caregiver"
"Soldier"	"Board Member"	"Mentor"
"Counselor"	"Chairperson"	"Pastor"
"Grandparent"	"Volunteer"	"Nurse"
"Doctor"	"Contributor"	"Role Model"
"Problem Solver"	"Officer"	"Service Provider"

... and whatever title YOU go by!

My Mom is a Leader

My Mom is a great leader. She is a leader at home and in our community, and at my school. She is the Girl Scout leader. She even lets me help make cookies for the brownie troop.

She is also a Nurse Practioner. She helps [people] who might not be able to see a Doctor. Sometimes she gives them stiches and vaccinations. Ouch!! She even helps the parents and shows them how to take care of their children. Then she talks to the children.

At home she cooks with us. She makes be best spaghetti! it's delicious!! On Sundays we go to church. Sometimes we go out to lunch with Sister Ginger. My mom also helps Sister Ginger by setting up for special partys. I think my mom is veary special and I love her! She has set an example for me by showing me how to always help others, She always takes the time to explin things to me.

My community is a better place to live because my mom is a kind and generous person.

~ Theresa Lobato
Student Essay Winner

Leadership is …

RESPECT

I'm not concerned with your liking or disliking me … All I ask is that you respect me as a human being.

~ JACKIE ROBINSON

If you have some respect for people as they are,
you can be more effective in helping them to
become better than they are.

~ John W. Gardner

We should question ourselves before we pass
judgment on someone who looks different,
behaves different, talks different, is a different color.

~ Johnny Depp

Leaders who win the respect of others are the
ones who deliver more than they promise, not the
ones who promise more than they can deliver.

~ Mark A. Clement

Men are respectable only as they respect.

~ Ralph Waldo Emerson

I believe every person has the ability to achieve
something important, and with that in mind I
regard everyone as special.

~ Mary Kay Ash

Respect is about how to treat everyone, not
just those you want to impress.

~ Richard Branson

You're better than no one and
no one is better than you.

~ Bob Dylan

"BASIC TRAINING" ON

R E S P E C T

RECOGNIZE the inherent worth of all human beings.

ELIMINATE derogatory words and phrases from your vocabulary.

SPEAK with people – not at them ... or about them.

PRACTICE empathy. Walk awhile in others' shoes.

EARN respect from others through respect-worthy behaviors.

CONSIDER others' feelings before speaking and acting.

TREAT everyone with dignity and courtesy.

~ WALK the TALK

Leadership is ...

RESPONSIBILITY

Rank does not confer privilege or give power.

It imposes responsibility.

~ PETER F. DRUCKER

In the long run, we shape our lives, and
we shape ourselves. The process never ends
until we die. And the choices we make
are ultimately our responsibility.

~ Eleanor Roosevelt

Man must cease attributing his problems to
his environment, and learn again to exercise
his will – his personal responsibility.

~ Albert Schweitzer

Leadership happens at every level of the
organization and no one can shirk
from this responsibility.

~ Jerry Junkins

It often happens that I wake up at night and begin
to think about a serious problem and decide
I must tell the Pope about it. Then I wake
up completely and remember that I am the Pope.

~ Pope John XXIII

We have the Bill of Rights.
What we need is a Bill of Responsibilities.

~ Bill Maher

When a man points a finger at someone else,
he should remember that four of his
fingers are pointing at himself.

~ Louis Nizer

Success on any major scale requires you to
accept responsibility. In the final analysis, the
one quality that all successful people have is
the ability to take on responsibility.

~ Michael Korda

One of the annoying things about believing in free
choice and individual responsibility is the difficulty
of finding someone to blame your problems on.
And when you do find somebody, it's
remarkable how often his picture turns up
on your driver's license.

~ P. J. O'Rourke

Leadership is …

RECOGNIZING
OTHERS

Everyone has an invisible sign

hanging from their neck saying:

Make me feel important!

~ MARY KAY ASH

Appreciation can make a day – even
change a life. Your willingness to put it into
words is all that is necessary.

~ Margaret Cousins

God gave you a gift of 86,400 seconds today.
Have you used one to say "thank you"?

~ William A. Ward

I can live for two months on one good compliment.

~ Mark Twain

People are not motivated by failure; they
are motivated by achievement and recognition.

~ F. Fournies

Most of us, swimming against the tides of
trouble the world knows nothing about,
need only a bit of praise or encouragement –
and we will make the goal.

~ Jerome P. Fleishman

I've always been a sucker for attention.

~ Cuba Gooding, Jr.

Nine-tenths of wisdom is APPRECIATION.
Go find somebody's hand and squeeze it …
while there's still time!

~ Dale Dauten

There are high spots in all of our lives
and most of them have come about through
encouragement from someone else.
I don't care how great, how famous or
successful a man or woman may be,
each hungers for applause.

~ George M. Adams

Leadership is …

SELF-CONTROL

Leadership is doing what is right
when no one is watching.

~ GEORGE VAN VALKENBURG

The best time for you to hold your tongue is
the time you feel you must say something or bust.

~ Josh Billings

The quality of a leader is reflected in the
standards they set for themselves.

~ Ray Kroc

Leaders do not have the luxury of ...

- acting on feelings rather than facts – jumping to
  conclusions and reacting in a "knee-jerk" fashion.

- forming opinions and making judgments knowing
  only one side of the story.

- wearing their emotions "on their sleeves."

Leadership is …

STRENGTH
AND COURAGE

*All our dreams can come true
if we have the courage to pursue them.*

~ WALT DISNEY

The ultimate measure of a man is not where he
stands in moments of comfort and convenience,
but where he stands at times of
challenge and controversy.

~ Martin Luther King, Jr.

Success is never final and failure never fatal.
It's courage that counts.

~ George F. Tilton

Strength does not come from winning.
Your struggles develop your strength. When
you go through hardships and decide
not to surrender, that is strength.

~ Arnold Schwarzenegger

Our greatest strength comes not from
what we possess, but from what we believe; not
from what we have, but from who we are.

~ Michael S. Dukakis

If I were asked to give what I consider
the single most useful bit of advice for
all humanity, it would be this:
Expect trouble as an inevitable part of life and
when it comes, hold your head high, look it squarely
in the eye and say, "I will be bigger than you.
You cannot defeat me."

~ Ann Landers

Courage is ...

Following your conscience instead of "following the crowd."

Refusing to take part in hurtful or disrespectful behaviors.

Sacrificing personal gain for the benefit of others.

Speaking your mind even though others don't agree.

Taking complete responsibility for your actions ...
and your mistakes.

Following the rules – and insisting that others do the same.

Challenging the status quo in search of better ways.

Doing what you know is right – regardless of the risks and
potential consequences.

~ WALK the TALK

Leadership is …
SERVICE

Leadership is an opportunity to serve.
It is not a trumpet call to self-importance.

~ J. DONALD WALTERS

There is no more noble occupation in
the world than to assist another
human being – to help someone succeed.

~ Alan Loy McGinnis

The first responsibility of a leader is to define
reality. The last is to say thank you. In
between, the leader is a servant.

~ Max DePree

My hope still is to leave this world a little
better for my being here.

~ Jim Henson

LEADERSHIP IN ACTION

Back in 2000, a young cancer patient was driven to do something very right … to demonstrate extraordinary leadership when it came to caring for others.

Her name was Alexandra ("Alex") Scott, and she came up with a rather simple idea: She would set up a lemonade stand and raise money to help find a cure for kids with cancer. So, with the help of her older brother, she assembled "Alex's Lemonade Stand for Childhood Cancer" on the front lawn of her home.

Although her health was deteriorating and her condition worsening, Alex continued to hold an annual lemonade sale for the next four years – with all of her "profits" going to childhood cancer research.

As a result of the inspirational example of this tiny young girl with a weak body but enormous heart, literally thousands of lemonade stands and other fundraising events have been held across the United States.

Sponsored by children, schools, businesses, and service organizations, these many activities benefit the **Alex's Lemonade Stand Foundation** for childhood cancer established by her family and many friends. As of 2007, the foundation had raised over $10 million for childhood cancer research.

On August 1st, 2004, "Alex" Scott died peacefully at the age of 8. While she will greatly be missed by all who knew her and knew of her, Alex's short yet unforgettable life truly is a celebration of the human spirit.

So, the next time you wonder if one person can make a difference, think of Alex – one little girl who literally took lemons and made lemonade; one little soul who inspires all of us to be leaders and serve others.

Note: For information on the
Alex's Lemonade Stand Foundation,
please visit alexslemonade.org.

Leadership is ...

HUMILITY

*Avoid putting yourself before others
and you can become a leader among men.*

~ Lao Tzu

It takes a great person to be truly humble,
and a humble person to be truly great.

~ Brian Gareau

If anything goes bad, I did it. If anything goes
semi-good, we did it. If anything goes really good,
then you did it. That's all it takes to get people
to win football games for you.

~ Paul "Bear" Bryant

Humility is not thinking less of yourself
but thinking of yourself less.

~ Unknown

Humility leads to strength and not to weakness.
It is the highest form of self-respect to
admit mistakes and to make amends for them.

~ John (Jay) McCloy

People who look down on other people
don't end up being looked up to.

~ Robert Half

Do you wish people to think well of you?
Don't speak well of yourself.

~ Blaise Pascal

Without humility there can be no humanity.

~ John Buchan

The leaders who work most effectively, it seems to me,
never say "I" … They don't think "I" – they think "we" …
They accept responsibility and don't sidestep it,
but "we" gets the credit. This is what creates trust,
what enables you to get the task done.

~ Peter Drucker

ARE YOU THE ANSWER?

If others were to ask "Are there any
humble people left in this
world?" would they be able to
point at you and say:
"Yes … we're looking at one right now!"?

Leadership is …

HONESTY

*Each time you are honest and conduct
yourself with honesty, a success force will drive
you toward greater success. Each time you
lie, even with a little white lie, there are strong
forces pushing you toward failure.*

~ JOSEPH SUGARMAN

Honesty is the cornerstone of all success,
without which confidence and ability to
perform shall cease to exist.

~ Mary Kay Ash

You'll never get mixed up if you simply tell
the truth. Then you don't have to
remember what you have said, and you
never forget what you have said.

~ Sam Rayburn

The truth is the kindest thing we
can give folks in the end.

~ Harriet Beecher Stowe

The best mind-altering drug is truth.

~ Lily Tomlin

I have found that being honest is the best technique
I can use. Right up front, tell people what
you're trying to accomplish and what you're
willing to sacrifice to accomplish it.

~ Lee Iacocca

Honesty and transparency make you vulnerable.
Be honest and transparent anyway.

~ Mother Teresa

Truth has no special time of its own.
Its hour is now – always.

~ Albert Schweitzer

A plaque is displayed at the entrance to the
Vanderbilt University Student Center which reads:

Today I am going to give you two examinations,
one in trigonometry and one in honesty.
I hope you will pass them both, but if you
must fail one, let it be trigonometry.

The center is named for the author of
that statement, Madison Sarratt, and was installed
in 1993 by the Undergraduate Honor Council.

Leadership is ...

HOPE

The first task of a leader is to keep hope alive.

~ JOE BATTEN

We must accept finite disappointment,
but never lose infinite hope.

~ Martin Luther King, Jr.

Of all the forces that make for a better world,
none is so indispensable, none so powerful,
as hope. Without hope men are only half alive.
With hope they dream and think and work.

~ Charles Sawyer

A leader is a dealer in hope.

~ Napoleon Bonaparte

The gift we can offer others is
so simple a thing as hope.

~ Daniel Berrigan

Leadership is …

INVOLVEMENT

I don't believe in just ordering
people to do things. You have to sort of
grab an oar and row with them.

~ HAROLD S. GENEEN

Delegating work works, provided the
one delegating works, too.

~ Robert Half

Lead me, follow me, or get out of my way!

~ Gen. George S. Patton

When I stand before God at the end
of my life, I would hope that I would not
have a single bit of talent left, and could
say, *I used everything you gave me.*

~ Erma Bombeck

Leadership is …

INSPIRATION

*A leader's role is to raise people's
aspirations for what they can
become and to release their energies
so they will try to get there.*

~ DAVID R. GERGEN

Leadership is the art of getting someone else to do something you want done because he wants to do it.

~ Dwight D. Eisenhower

We have to undo a 100-year-old concept and convince our managers that their role is not to control people and stay on top of things, but rather to guide, energize, and excite.

~ Jack Welch

Keep your fears to yourself, but share your inspiration with others.

~ Robert Louis Stevenson

If people are coming to work excited …
if they're making mistakes freely and
fearlessly … if they're having fun … if they're
concentrating on doing things … then
somewhere you have leaders.

~ Robert Townsend

Leadership is not so much about technique
and methods as it is about opening
the heart. Leadership is about
inspiration – of oneself and of others.
Great leadership is about human
experiences, not processes. Leadership is
not a formula or a program, it is a
human activity that comes from the heart
and considers the hearts of others.

~ Lance Secretan

A "Crash Course" on
INSPIRATIONAL LEADERSHIP

The 10 most important words: *"What can I do to help you be more successful?"*

The 9 most important words: *"We need to do this, and here is why ...."*

The 8 most important words: *"That's my mistake and I will fix it."*

The 7 most important words: *"My door is always open to you."*

The 6 most important words: *"Let's focus on solving the problem."*

The 5 most important words: *"You did a great job!"*

The 4 most important words: *"What do YOU think?"*

The 3 most important words: *"Follow my example."*

The 2 most important words: *"Thank You."*

The **MOST** important word: *"YOU"*

Leadership is …

INTEGRITY

I think leadership comes from integrity –
that you do whatever you ask others to do …
Just by providing a good example as a parent, a friend,
a neighbor makes it possible for other people to see
better ways to do things.

~ Scott Berkun

Leadership is a potent combination of strategy
and character. But if you must be
without one, be without the strategy.

~ Gen. Norman Schwarzkopf

Integrity is not a 90 percent thing, not a
95 percent thing; either you have it or you don't.

~ Peter Scotese

Real integrity is doing the right thing, knowing
that nobody's going to know whether you did it or not.

~ Oprah Winfrey

So live that you wouldn't be ashamed
to sell the family parrot to the town gossip.

~ Will Rogers

LEADERSHIP IN ACTION

While installing a jack for a customer, Frank Walmsley, a multimedia services technician with Verizon Connected Solutions in Newport News, Virginia, had to go up into the small attic space above the customer's bedroom.

Frank found several open boxes in the crawl space and told the customer that one of the boxes contained cash. After Frank brought the box down, the customer offered some of the money to Walmsley as a finder's fee. He politely declined. When Frank finished the job, the customer again offered Walmsley a tip. Again, he politely declined, said thank you, and left a card.

"Every time you go into a customer's home, you're in a position of trust," Frank said. "Customers see 'Verizon' and they know they can trust us, and you've got to have respect for that."

Walmsley's supervisor, Steve Imsande, wasn't surprised to learn of his technician's integrity in refusing the money.

"Every hour of every day, you have a decision to make," he said. "You can either make the right decision or the wrong one. Frank is just one of those guys who figures he's got a job to do and he's going to do it the right way."

Source: Verizon Corporate Website

ARE YOU THE ANSWER?

If others were to ask "Are there any role models
of integrity that our children can learn from?"
would they be able to point at you and say:
"Indeed … there's someone who walks the talk!"?

Leadership is …

PATIENCE

The practice of patience toward one another,
the overlooking of one another's defects,
and the bearing of one another's burdens is
the most elementary condition of all human
and social activity in the family, in the
professions, and in society.

~ LAWRENCE G. LOVASIK

Patience is the art of caring slowly.

~ John Ciardi

The key to everything is patience.
You get the chicken by hatching the egg,
not by smashing it open.

~ Arnold H. Glasgow

Sometimes it helps to know that
I just can't do it all. One step at a time is all that's possible –
even when those steps are taken on the run.

~ Anne W. Schaef

Patience, persistence and perspiration
make an unbeatable combination for success.

~ Napoleon Hill

Learn the art of patience. Apply discipline
to your thoughts when they become
anxious over the outcome of a goal. Impatience
breeds anxiety, fear, discouragement and
failure. Patience creates confidence, decisiveness,
and a rational outlook, which eventually leads to success.

~ Brian Adams

If I'm not back in five minutes ... just wait longer!

~ Ace Ventura, *Pet Detective*

Fact is ...

Not everyone you interact with will be as smart as you.

Not everyone you serve will know what they want or really need.

Not everyone you work with will be as talented or as quick as you.

Not everyone you lead will know what you know – or feel what you feel.

Not everyone on the team will have the same sense of urgency as you.

Not everyone in your group will share your energy and excitement.

Some people will make more honest mistakes than you will.

Some people will need more help than you do.

Some people will be dealing with more problems and issues than you are.

So, how do you deal with these facts of life?
You do it by "cutting others a little slack";
you do it by being understanding – and avoiding
responsive behaviors that make people feel bad,
inadequate, or just plain stupid.

That's patience ... **that's** LEADERSHIP!

Leadership is …

PASSION

*I can't imagine a person becoming a success
who doesn't give this game of life everything he's got.*

~ WALTER CRONKITE

Without passion, a person will have very
little influence as a leader.

~ Michele Payn-Knoper

Unless someone like you cares a whole
awful lot, nothing is going to get better, it's not.

~ Dr. Seuss

We may affirm absolutely that nothing great in the world
has ever been accomplished without passion.

~ Georg Hegel

We could hardly wait to get up in the morning.

~ Wilbur Wright

An effective leader is a person with a
passion for a cause that is larger
than they are. Someone with a dream
and a vision that will better society,
or at least, some portion of it.

~ Sandra Larson

SURGEON GENERAL'S WARNING:

Passion is highly contagious and can lead to improved

performance, greater satisfaction, and the creation

of positive differences.

Nothing is as important as passion.
No matter what you want to do with your life,
be passionate.

~ Jon Bon Jovi

It is really important that young people find something
that they want to do and pursue it with passion.

~ Spike Lee

And life is what we make it. Always has been, always will be.

~ Grandma Moses

When you're in your nineties and looking back,
it's not going to be how much money you made or
how many awards you've won. It's really what did you stand for.
Did you make a positive difference for people?

~ Elizabeth Dole

Leadership is …

PEOPLE

Leadership is all about people.
It is not about organizations. It is not about plans.
It is not about strategies. It is all about people –
motivating people to get the job done.
You have to be people-centered.

~ COLIN POWELL

One measure of leadership is the
caliber of people who choose to follow you.

~ Dennis Peer

Leadership is the special quality which
enables people to stand up and
pull the rest of us over the horizon.

~ James L. Fisher

When the leadership is right and the
time is right, the people can always be counted
upon to follow – to the end at all costs.

~ Harold J. Seymour

Leadership is not magnetic personality –
that can just as well be a glib tongue.
It is not "making friends and influencing people" – that is flattery.
Leadership is lifting a person's vision to higher sights,
the raising of a person's performance to a higher standard,
the building of a personality beyond its normal limitations.

~ Peter F. Drucker

Our most basic common link is that we all inhabit
this small planet. We all breathe the same air. We all cherish
our children's future. And we are all mortal.

~ John F. Kennedy

If you don't think of yourself as a leader,
then you're limited in your thinking.
Leading is the way we help move people
into action, including ourselves. The question is
not whether you are a leader,
but how well you lead.

~ BRUCE D. SCHNEIDER

About the Authors

STEVE VENTURA is a respected author, book producer, and award-winning training program designer. His work reflects over 30 years of human resource development experience – both as a practitioner and a business consultant. His prior books include: *Start Right ... Stay Right*, *Walk Awhile In My Shoes*, *Five Star Teamwork*, *Conflict Happens*, *LEAD RIGHT*, and *WALK the TALK*. *Leadership Lessons* is the fifth work he has co-authored with Eric Harvey.

ERIC HARVEY, president and founder of WalkTheTalk.com, is a leading expert on Ethics and Values-Based Practices. He is a renowned business consultant and the author of thirty highly acclaimed books – including the best-selling *WALK the TALK*, *Ethics4Everyone* and *The Leadership Secrets of Santa Claus*. He and his team of professionals have helped thousands of individuals and organizations turn their values into value-added results.

Take *Leadership Lessons* to the next level with the
LEAD RIGHT LIBRARY!

A complete library of 14 best-selling leadership resources.
Tackling leadership topics such as coaching, recognition,
communication, and ethics, this library contains everything
that you need to lead right. Whether you are a senior
manager or just starting out your professional career ...
these books are for you!

Visit WalkTheTalk.com for more information.

Introducing FREE online newsletters from
WalkTheTalk.com

❖ **Customer Service Monday Morning Must-Read:** Practical tips to increase customer satisfaction, loyalty, and retention.

❖ **The Power of Inspiration:** Designed to uplift, inspire, and motivate you and the important people in your life.

❖ **212° Midweek Motivator:** Midweek motivation inspiring you to achieve results beyond your wildest expectations.

❖ **Leadership Lessons:** Weekly tips to help you and your colleagues become more effective and respected leaders.

❖ **Daily Motivation:** Powerful messages to "kick start" your day.

WalkTheTalk.com newsletters are designed to motivate, inform, and inspire you to reach new levels of skills and confidence!

Visit WalkTheTalk.com to sign up
for these powerful newsletters!

About the Publisher

Since 1977, The WALK THE TALK Company (WalkTheTalk.com) has helped individuals and organizations, worldwide, achieve success through Values-Based Practices. Our goal is both simple and straightforward: to provide you and your organization with high-impact resources for your personal and professional success!

We specialize in:

- ❖ How-To Handbooks and Support Material
- ❖ Inspirational Books and Movies
- ❖ Motivational Newsletters
- ❖ Group Training Programs
- ❖ Do-It-Yourself Resources
- ❖ 360° Feedback Processes

  And Much More!

Contact us to learn more:
WalkTheTalk.com
1100 Parker Square, Suite 250
Flower Mound, TX 75028
info@walkthetalk.com
888.822.9255

128

If you think "leadership" is a concept that only applies
to certain people in business, governmental, and
civic organizations, think again!
Fact is – no matter our age, gender, occupation,
education level, or station in life –
each of us touches and influences other lives …

EACH OF US IS A LEADER TO *SOMEONE*.

That's why LEADERSHIP is something we all must be
concerned with. That's why the lessons presented
in this book apply to each of us …

THAT'S WHY THEY APPLY TO *YOU*.

WALKTHETALK.COM

Resources for Personal and Professional Success